REPUBLIC OF MERCY

THE KUNDIMAN PRIZE

An annual award with publication of a poetry collection by an Asian American poet, selected by the artistic staff of Kundiman and the editors of Tupelo Press.

Kundiman creates an affirming and rigorous space where Asian American writers can explore, through art, the unique challenges that face the new and ever-changing diaspora. We see the arts as a tool of empowerment, of education and liberation, addressing proactively what legacy we will leave for our future generations as individuals and as a community.

PREVIOUS WINNERS

The Cowherd's Son by Rajiv Mohabir (Tupelo Press)
Driving Without a License by Janine Joseph (Alice James Books)
Yearling by Lo Kwa Mei-en (Alice James Books)
Split by Cathy Linh Che (Alice James Books)
Mezzanines by Matthew Olzmann (Alice James Books)
Pier by Janine Oshiro (Alice James Books)

REPUBLIC OF MERCY

Sharon Wang

TUPELO PRESS

North Adams, Massachusetts

Library of Congress Cataloging-in-Publication Data
Names: Wang, Sharon, 1989- author.
Title: Republic of mercy / Sharon Wang.
Description: First paperback edition. | North Adams, Massachusetts : Tupelo
  Press, [2018] | The Kundiman Poetry Prize.
Identifiers: LCCN 2018013984 | ISBN 9781946482129 (pbk. original : alk. paper)
Classification: LCC PS3623.A3688 A6 2018 | DDC 811/.6--dc23

Cover and text designed and composed in Bodoni Book by Howard Klein.

First paperback edition: October 2018.

Tupelo Press
P.O. Box 1767, North Adams, Massachusetts 01247
(413) 664-9611/editor@tupelopress.org/www.tupelopress.org

Tupelo Press is an award-winning independent literary press that publishes
fine fiction, nonfiction, and poetry in books that are a joy to hold as well as
read. Tupelo Press is a registered 501(c)(3) nonprofit organization, and we rely
on public support to carry out our mission of publishing extraordinary work
that may be outside the realm of the large commercial publishers. Financial
donations are welcome and are tax deductible.

for Anton Khlevitt

CONTENTS

THREE

Wasp Ode

FOUR

FIVE

STORY

We knew before the thing
happened but what good did it do.
Like learning/ a nursery rhyme,
reciting, he was a good horse.
Branches bending/ then flowers,
a flash occurred. We must have
looked up. Sounds, low,
and the swaying of each sound—
they felt like sightings of
one dark animal, then another,
breaking up a line of hills.
I heard each syllable, discernible
and discrete. If there is any sort
of order in, say, a hand placing
flowers down into the room
a light crashes into. If an act tugs
another act the way the moon
tugs at threads of water. And threads
of water tug at a surface/ netted,
rippling, fallible mirror, false surface
in which limbs could submerge
under black and rolling liquid.
I breathed into his open mouth,
I think. One of us tossed a pebble,
a stranger observed where it struck.

ONE

MICROPHONES, BREAD, AND LOVE

In brutality
I found a beauty wholly other
from that of a woman walking
across a room
to rearrange flowers.

You could say it was itself
the flower,
a bloom in an eye

and for which I practiced movements
the way a songbird rehearses its

frenetic crests and troughs in its head
all night

before they grow full against air.

ELEGY ON WHITE

There is no consolation
in an object that is beautiful.
No consolation in an object that is not.
Soul is alien
to the order of flesh and trees.

I have pressed my ear
to another human and found nothing
but white noise,
and even then what I heard
was the wiring of blood
being thrown through a torso.

SWAN SONG/FALTER/

When the bells changed, I put them
in his mouth

I put my hands over

Something shaking within
that noise/ as if
our hands were leaves/ our arms
branches

If breath could make/ a peak
a hook, an arrow, a missive

Something was lost
We stared at each other
as if we were
the field where it was last rumored
to have been seen

IF WE COULD

If we could raise a cry
and it could spill a shadow
that widens
to overtake all the sprays of leaves—

We made a spoke pushed
from our center,
a wheel pressed into dirt,
spokes spinning broad and firm
until we did not know how to greet
our new spaces (flashing,
tender), while a loom clicked
and all the soft thread was plied
and stretched, into what

Sometimes a Cry Fell in the Night

A violence,
like a petal,
was pinned into place.

We slid a knife
between the shoulders,
cut a ribbon
that held the body,
reduced ourselves
to rubble.

Once my mouth
touched a body
with the pressure of a pin.

When I came to
I was surrounded
by leaves.

One leaf had
an edgeless hole
which I could make
a noise through
with my lips.

Inside You Music Stops

Did you comb the world to ask
who made each thing
that you were compelled
to find beautiful
even when things had gone wrong.

I am shining my thoughts onto
you, pouring incandescent artificial light onto

a canvas of skin.

(

I confuse emptiness
and crying
with hunger.

It must be possible to dig through
the center of the earth and reach

a clearing

ELEGY FOR ALLOWANCE

I made a shroud in the mouth.

Light, but heavier than what I could hope to keep.

As if I'd stolen something, and,
just as a person turned my way,

had pushed the thing into my mouth.

And the punishment was to never
show it to anyone.

HERE

Soul enters flesh
so forcefully

the way a hand clenched into a fist
too long thrusts opens, numb.

Bed of Aster

Between the visible world and
the invisible is a slit, sharp as a cut
made by a thin-edged leaf
drawn across skin. Or a knife wielded
between the two bundles of the mind.

Here white flowers are open—

(with a threading inside them, asking
them to open, shut, *live*.)

Inside each flower
is a center
that the eye can press towards endlessly
without ever precisely knowing.

The more I look,
the less I feel I know.

Practice in the Shadow Room

To call the body occupied, one had to first occupy—
wire suspended in an empty room.

Nothing perched on it.

When I touched him again I didn't feel
his body, exactly,
but some shape of it held in mind,
the way I held the pears,
whose forms were outlined in light.

Rolling until we'd forgotten
they were called pear.

He said, *we have to get to the core of it,*
and we sharpened our knives across the loins.

Gourd-flower, flesh-flower, what passed into
the bird's mouth and came away, cleaned.
What passed beneath the knife, the hand knowing how.

Deep inside the fruit: the cross-cut
of a hidden star.

SEE HOW

the light moves through
small rings of leaves,
making flashes on the ruffled
necks of birds. Hold

the branch out farther and it does not
disturb the trees, although birds
fly away in a small burst, a star
of birds, or a flower widening
so quickly it would bend at the stem.

I think this tree. Its grooves
are thin to the eye but deep
to the hand, as if it has pulled
inside itself, pulled
inside deeply, and closed over.

The mind touches hardly anything at all.

PERFECTIBLE WORLD (1)

There was a melancholy
that could only be pressed by others,
so when we tried
to press it ourselves,
it only grew more undrinkable.

The more we drank the more
we began to bend, until we were
the cattle not knowing
what it was to want
such kindness.

Once, I touched my hand
to his back and smoke
came away in my hand.

I said, *sorry*, and he said,
No it was the chimney, the poplars.
The nest of starlings coming loose
on this side of the fence.

TWO

Squinting, It Was Hard to Tell

When the first of the longings left,
it came back months later, with only
a tooth missing. She gave it food.
It began to sing. It was only when they
all began to go missing that she started
to worry. She was not accustomed
to worry. She felt that she was not
very practiced, and in perfecting it
she might often make mistakes.
More so than the missing, it was
the mistaking that worried her.
Where were they, she wondered,
now free of their cooings in the night.
How were they doing, with plenty
of strange bodies to feed them.

LULLABY

Here, little girl. Here,
this world, round as a tube of cream.

You rub it on your hand and the friction lessens;
you rub it on and the surface goes soft.

Like nursing a tooth, the feeling never disappears.

Here is the enclosure. Here is the hinge.
You are the carapace and *here* is irreducible.

It is the cornea and you a menagerie of curiosities.

Close your eyes. Close your eyes.
A silver guillotine falls.

Everything on this side of it is hard and brilliant.

Everything on the other side is soft
and beckons you to touch.

The softer it is,
the more you want to touch.

Ashes, ashes, you roll in the heap of others.

And you are here and you are gone.

Misalignment

Just a bit of glass in the eye:
that's what the boy thought,

and then the glass reached his
heart. A bit of glass, turning, the turn
itself a bloom,

its own gyre and eye. Steeple and scalpel,
everything compressed and rotated

in its original image, the hanged man in his
boat of bog.

In the miscellanea of
grotesques, all was curious,

the misshapen bee, the clutched rose,
even her face—

the world made astonishing.

He loved the world. He loved it suddenly
and without reason.

It was a burr on the mind that he
regarded fondly,

its stinging a small and inexact fee.

AXIOMS

This is what was memorized:

Glass is more transparent
than wood and air even more transparent
than glass.

A dot an inch from the right and a dot
an inch from the left
can be brought together by folding:
an elimination of space.

The end song of a tree is slower than
the end song of a mechanical grasshopper.

If you hold a sugar cube in your hand,
sometimes a man will eat from it.

Meanwhile they grew light.
They didn't even know it.

They could have walked into the sickle lake
with a pitcher of milk and that alone
would have been enough to sink them.

LIKE SOMETHING STITCHING THE AIR TO ITSELF

She looked into a mirror
and saw her eyes with an X
of light inside, splitting
the pupils with force. As if
her own gaze could kill her.
And then later they were just
two things cushioned
in an amniotic case, surrounded
by flourishing serifs and the floating
and poised small heads of letters
that indicated autonomy (or,
self-effacement). So much left
unsaid that it wrapped
around them, soft, and like a shroud,
and you could weave it into
something, she thought,
maybe, or maybe the weaving
was the violence itself,
another disorder.

GRAPHITE

They were rubble horses
who thought
they were real horses.

A whinny signaled another
whinny,
each an aster
in the cochlea.

> World scalded with silence
> and filaments   of noise.

In the lattice-
field they
shifted, nuzzling shame
from someone's hand.

CINEMA

Like a floater fading in an eye,
the heroine passed through the universe

not knowing anything
of grandness.

One by one
her mitochondria rebelled

and had to be convinced
of a greater order.

PERFECTIBLE WORLD (2)

When a sheet pressed against his face
it kept no indentation as it pulled away.

He was only a flight
of blood in migration again and again,
and when I touched him I couldn't disappear.

The sunlight longing over our mouths
knew us the way I knew
my own body when I explored the interior
not out of pleasure
but inevitability.

Imagine being the sun
and still unable to see or comprehend.

But who wouldn't want to be the sun.

All my life I wanted
to be bright, and shining.

Held people in my brain until
they became dark mounds

to make incisions in. A cut,
an unzipping. A light arising

from the loosening shadow-burlap.

The best thing in its category
is a secret. The prettiest sister

dusted by several eons of cinder.
Kind people compelled to absolute silence.

Imagine a love folding into itself,
a white gull folding until

there is almost nothing but white.
The flash of ochre in its beak

hidden so deeply
inside a shift of feathers

that no eye can fetch it out.

We kissed with the curtains open
and lights off, the outside air falling
as swiftly as dots placed on a page,
dots making shapes that could lift
from picture if only you looked
with a certain kind of attention,
if you believed
that a shape made of dots
was really a shape.

Extra linen pinned to the back of someone's
curtain, crowding into ruffles.
If the pins loosened, what would that be,
one fold cascading over another,
something hardly contained.

THREE

WASP ODE

Herself

Look: wool makes sparks over the eyes
if chafed

        across skin at a certain

speed. In a flash, one can see

        everything, before becoming again
        submerged.

Once, I built my looking-glass out of wire
and weft.
        I waited until obfuscation

distressed me, knowing as I did
how to make it

mine. I could no longer place my own
        nature,

        carried my losses like a dark
red flower, as if a flower were

a tourniquet for the branch
        that made it,
each petal bent back and layered
like shale.

I carried two trees like torches, one within the torso,
the other within the mind. And the roots of one

spread in the world as the other held me
to the ground, kept me there . . .

> I held onto people who were missing and to

> things unmade by people

(A flower blooms. I cry.
I walk to the store to buy bread in the mornings.)

The Other

Yes, she looked like me, the girl who called herself by
what she was in relation to others.

She appeared sometimes in the corners of reflections,

in the plate of water I had left out in the flat for three days
in the curve of the transistor radio I was given on my third birthday
in the door that I passed through to get to my place of work.

I could see her flickering. I knew her.

The way she held her hands apart when she wanted
to hide something, the manner in which she cried.

(

In the Republic of Mercy, we had come to understand
that objects change each others' properties in space:

that atoms tug and shift each other in space:

that the innate characteristics of each object are marked only by
a complicated lattice of compulsion and repulsion:

that, in tandem, compulsion and repulsion form the shapes
called human, bird, tumbler, xylophone.

(

When she cried, I was compelled.

When she moved her hands, I was repulsed.

When I moved my hands too, she was always gone.

Herself

Sometimes, there was a screen, through which it was possible

 to see all things:

                the crests, the troughs, the strange

oases in which moss could lick the body, rear to neck,

and there would be some rupture; a sound, perhaps,

a slab of light that slid through an opening and worked its way in,

hardened and whole, clarified—

                        so for a moment,

I'd be jolted, and her too, looking in the back of the glass

to find what could be seen out of the corners of the eye,

a shadow through a cataract:

        I saw the world first through a slit

        then I was the aberration

The Other

We had, following other discoveries,

synced up particular voices to particular physiognomies:

particular gestures to particular emotions:

everything equalized as to marginalize room for harm.

Harm had its own rooms, in the Grand Mausoleums
beneath the city center.

Prescribed visiting hours for the curious were 9 to noon.

An ex-boyfriend claimed to have stolen a steel cat
from the corridors, tied it up with wire,

and had it re-programmed to recite Keats in a staccato voice
when he had intelligentsia over.

Another friend said she met her fiancé there.

Probably neither of them had ever even seen
the inside of that place.

Herself

I'd stretched a sheet out over the screen, like a curtain

in a morgue. Every once in a while trees made shadow puppetry

through it, slim with their slim shapes which I could not grapple
or feud,

feeding them as I did to the ambient dark and things

that lurked in it, like feeding scraps to a scrappy dog you want

to grow larger, whose teeth come to scrape across the sinew

of the heart and calves in gratitude, in composure. When
one thing

came, there was always another, a series of bright lights
answering

each others' calls, watchtowers on a phantom fissure. This was
my life.

And sometimes a thing would go missing.

The Other

In year twenty of the Republic of Mercy there came to be built
a glass-bottomed boat that could fit half the people

of the nation, exactly half. In it you could
travel, go places, see fish in their many-finned splendor.

Above: a large wood dome. Flat, dark,
the bodies fitted into each space like coins in a slot.

I took the boat for many rotations, traveled in my sleep,
marveled at the ingenuity of the burrs that turned,

always propelling the thing forward, not leaving us to rest.
Below: the infinite world,

all its ligaments, all its creatures.

Herself

And each time a thing went missing there was

an aftermark, a singe that could be sensed only if

I happened to brush right up against the edge of it,

like a dog against a leg, or an elephant scurrying around

a dime. If I pushed into the center of it

there was only a whiff of a memory, marking what

I should have known, as a pear-shaped mark on wood

comes to stand in for pear or something that just looked

like it, something much larger—

The Other

When a signal sent collided with a signal from the receiver,
the peaks and valleys could easily skew,
and all of the frequencies occurred at all the wrong times.

Therefore I had trouble understanding her, the girl from beyond.

But I always knew
the tap of the rhythm, learned it in my sleep, could reproduce
it without really understanding. Tap *tap* tap. Tap tap *tap tap*.

A message like a mistake you make so many times
it becomes ritual rather than accident,

or something you appropriate into a private lexicon,
say, the eye of an iris, so bright and large

it comes to represent sorrow, or drowning.
A marble placed in the mouth.

When you look away it is once again *iris*.

Like that, but over and over.

The Other

Like something misplaced followed by the tap that responds
to the silence carved out by it.

You know how sometimes a person you love walks off
the balcony one day, and the next day you can
just go on living your life?

Then months later you're reading something completely random
but it has the word "pressure-hook" in it,
and you start crying nonsensically.

Or you write a letter to your mother and it's lost in the currents
of a solar-storm. Then the repair agencies go: "soon,
communications will resume, soon . . ." And *soon*
comes to stand in for the thing you meant to tell her.

Herself

Because I had, in order to make sense out of nonsense,

begun to make a compendium: what to maim, who to trust.

Because violence was necessary to seeing

something truly, as when a parent tosses a lamp across a room

and for a moment before breaking, it makes the other objects

in the room careen across the walls.

I wanted to understand the properties of how things broke:

what it looked like, what it meant. If it wasn't possible to build

the world anew. What atoms, what ligaments I would then

be building from. Love as not a phantom hand reaching over

a phantom hand, but rather, something in the world;

not an object but a directionality for other forces of motion.

The Other

When I was a little kid, my mother made me an anagram
game to keep me occupied when no one was around.

You can do it with anything, she said.
Try starting with *wode-sparrow*.

She might have said wood-sparrow,
I think I heard it wrong.

When I was lonely I would start repeating it to myself,
permutating it. And only later did I realize that
the choices were fairly limited:

wode-sparrow, wasp-ode, sorrow-ape.

Yes, it became a staving off of enclosure,
an ordering of nonsense,

a rasping noise that lingered everywhere in the world.

Herself

Once, I made my looking-glass
out of wire and weft.

I carried my losses like a dark red flower,
as if a flower were

                  a tourniquet
for the thing that made it, each petal layered

       and bent back like shale...
Outside the trees clicked

as wind moved   through the flat wood-
tokens that people had hung in them,

as if they could ward out harm or
keep in what

could harm within reason.

(I stretch out a hand to the screen, touch
the other one—

       try to cross—)

FOUR

PERFECTIBLE WORLD (3)

We were the cattle/ not knowing what it was to want such kindness

Yes yes now our hoofs are dangling
crushed grasses   thin bent
beneath

move

here move slowly we are not   practiced

(

have you fed   yes   will you prod the
grasses   yes   take care among
the birds they tell false news   yes
take care among the rushes it is not quite
certain what they do although   yes
they purport to do it daily

how   bending unbending

(

look, we can mimic their bending
see, right hoof forward   right hoof   right
then left
then circle

(

look, the circle of grass when we
first came   became   first
we came here   look

white stones   sunlight
bright as the tint of
a meniscus   I remember

remember   yes   the water   yes
and the tenterhooks   yes yes
the noise that left the mouth as
a scarf flicking around in a circle
before escaping   that also

(

noise like a sleeve flicking around
a doorknob   but louder   noise
of something coming   loose
bones stitching tight crumpling
before we had a chance   to cry out
and then herded here   I am

(

here   remember the noises
we made   which ones
I tried to talk to you   yes

I said, say something   what   anything just
say something   then what

noises   sounded like
water tumbling in a hollow
log   roundness
holding no form   water   yes

crashing   on a bed
of water

remember how it was

(

and the ones we used
to make

trace a hoof around it what
remember   what
once, I said I will break you I traced
a finger across your mouth

my   yes   my mouth

(

what was that thing called   starling
no no that other thing   anvil

what about the one I used to scoop into
your mouth

spoon   no, it was ours
hands

SPRING RITUALS

A woman I admire gives me a stone. I am given a stone, and I can't parse the meaning.

I like the feeling of hoisting a bag of stones up—the contents shift, and there seems to be a choice between lifting the bag and keeping myself steady.

ELEGY FOR THE SPLENDID THING

Once I put my hand
to a fire and my hand survived
but not the fire.

Knotted and white, it became
a stump of a fire, a lily
in a natural history museum.

I put myself in a bathtub on the ocean
and pushed.

Water like the gleam
on a scalpel I turned in my head.

A person I loved fell into an ocean
and did not reappear.

Passing by my lily in my ocean
I saw it grow tendrils
and then spark plugs latching
to the jagged rocks,
forming an inscrutable
new anatomy.

ONCE, I WALKED WITH A MAN INTO A FIELD

We felt the cool air gather.
Each held a branch in one hand.
Watched the branches catch
and deflect light,
and even when placed in water
they did not appear broken,
not truly.

We'd lit the branches and placed
them close to our torsos.
To illuminate our bodies to
ourselves, only.
It wasn't a sort of beauty that
I wanted to even share with others.
It was like undressing with great care
and completely in the dark. Not
handing the branch to anyone
but simply holding it out.

Mea Culpa Elegy

I thought I could hone my mind until
intellect and emotion were
a single organ. The way a snake's motion
comes from the musculature
of its entire body, and when it moves
there is no part of it that
has not moved.
            I wanted to make you
something beautiful. As if I could
strike a branch against a word and make it
break into water: each syllable round,
and clenching, and then letting go finally
what it sought to claim.

Red Velvet Confessional

Is it possible to sleep far too often?
I do. When I wake it is too bright,

then too dark, then too bright again.
Soft and easy to stroke: the bed,

offering no resistance. I dream.
Steel, starting, aster:

things having nothing to do with me
hurt me. Spruce,

pointing towards sky. The sound "spruce,"
like the sensation of a knife slicing

through agar. Just soft enough
of an incision to imagine it going through

something with less give—

I wake with my head inside a snake's mouth.
The snake is arching, prescient.
Someone comes with a hammer
to strike its head.

I have wanted to feel that I
am worth something. The way a sheep
has worth, sheared for the winter
warming, its white flame of wool coaxed
into something of use.

Each helper with a hoof in one hand
holding tight the white thing as
it squirms, tries to kick free into
the stark landscape, blind need
tumbling forth with the urgency
of animal resistance.

I hold still my head
under a faucet.

I touch my neck: damp.
Matted hair releases
more droplets than I think.
Neck gives way
under water, water.

There is no truer way
to know a body
than under adverse circumstances.

Like listening to the falter
of a clockwork whose gears bite
into the wrong parts.

The saw-toothed grind goes and goes.

Fish all go one way
in a soft silt, their bodies
growing obscured yet traceable.

So often I have wanted
to place myself in danger,

past the point of salvation,
as if it would make my frantic

mind reasonable.
I dream I am a martyr,

circle the kitchen all day,
fill my body with rice and spices

for the kill. I walk the space
over and over, with an urgency

that seems to come from nothing,
silk scarf from a red sleeve

of failure—

and I, falling in an open field,

am no more
the field/ which amplifies
in patterns of bent grass

motions of the field mice
that pass through/ motions of
the wind/ that passes through

I am no more that
than the bullets/ are each

a widening/ pinhole of light

LIKE A HOOK

Like a hook passing
through an eye   it was necessary
to become small

The earth believed in *aster*, the way it breaks
up through dirt with a name
like an opening

star

Elegy Addressed (Atom Cloud, Hand)

At the end of the needle: the eye.

At the end of the eye: smoky pirouettes of swans
in a turned lake, robed in their black angers.

If you were in the ruins and the ruins inside you were a lake.

If you swam in the lake of your ruined mind, bullet
and umbilical, biting down time,

biting it clean as the widening field of inquiry
in a bright telescope,

the view at the end of a diminishing city.

This is the one to end all dreams.

A hunger so large it stops the mouth.

We wrap up the dreamer in giant leaves
before tossing him into the river.

The villagers say,
"The fish are ravenous."

They say, "But don't hold back."
"It doesn't matter if they don't leave much
because after all
you can keep nothing."

A great wave comes to lick
clean the gnats

in the bed of the dreamer.

You are

a sparrow shell that something
made a tiny hole in to suck the yolk out.

You are
the overturned train
inside the shell: red-velvet seats, bits
peeled off and stuck to the sides
of the track,
which is twisted and wrapped
out and around like someone's hair—

as if a mouth put to one silver line
could pitch a sound across and over,

until everything was covered
in that single small noise.

And if the town inside you
were burning
and the women and children were
balls rolling in a rubber ring
and you could pull out a single person
which person would you choose?
Duck, duck, goose.
You know how this goes.
Maybe you're like the stethoscope
without the doctor.
Or the rubber flower that comes to
stand in for the flower.
That's like the song I'm making for you.
I confuse you with everyone else
I meant to save, or love.

This is what I'd like to tell you.

I don't know how/ to take care
of anyone.

Imagine/ a woman crossing into herself
so deeply/ that even animals

used to burrowing in winter
can no longer
sense her presence.

And sometimes when I love a/ boy

I want to take him inside/ my arms the way
a seam swallows a dark spreading mark.

I want to blow his irises black.

And I want/ to coax the flower
the carmine/ flower

until it closes on the insect that's made its
home/ inside it,

the brilliant glass beetle that knows no
other/ world than this one.

Then we topple, two pins in the middle
of a jellyfish diaspora.

Even now, I do not know how
to go through with this procedure.
I'd rather let the entire stem
of the body atrophy than cut off
a single hand. Here, in the room,
I lick the threads so that the two bits fuse,
then blow them clean. Sun makes a halo
behind the hand-held mirror. The mirror
is cold on the side I face, plate of flame
on the other. My face is clear.

How do I let go, if I'm not willing
to leave anything behind?

Meanwhile the world comes off
your petrified flesh like pearls.

Overhead is a cloud of cumulus flowers.

It's hard to negotiate a private and
unsubstantial grief.

It's like putting on the wrong body
by mistake.

It's like crossing into air and not knowing
what you're making the crossing for.

Me, too.

Me too, and here I am nodding with you,
I'm propping your head back up.

The antler blooms on the body took over the entire

—if, indeed, it could have been called
                    the entire—

what left you first came back as a crash,
pushing through the waves, not wanting to give you up
I didn't want to give you up

in all the cymbals, there was only the great force

under great constraint, love comes, tumbling, through
large crests of   the filigree of

            Or what came after then, folding
and buckling as

the weeping cranes, with tips that sweep
            to the side among reeds

might find a place between sun
and hydrangea   bird   and sea

FIVE

Sorrow Ape

Sorrow without
genealogy or child. Mind,
a topiary with leaves sheared
and observed.
Some days, mind takes the tops
off all the flora.

Declares a new world order
of the beheaded.
Who have looked into the center
of the universe and found.
Rests on a parapet
pondering desire.
Thorn, heart.

Gazes at the body—

Through a mirror, above
a tub, where it lies.

I get close to memory.

Not close.

A person gathers, up,
into a tautness, a tear—unified,

almost spilling.

Acknowledgments

Thanks to Tupelo and to my editors: Jim Schley, Kristina Marie Darling.

Thanks to my workshop mates, for reading the infant iterations of these poems: Lawrence Ypil, Kerin Sulock, Luke Cumberland, Aditi Machado.

Thanks, Carl Phillips and Mary Jo Bang, for being first readers for an early, early draft of this book.

Thanks to my first teachers, Jorie Graham and Joanna Klink, for making the world feel so rich.

Thank you to my first-ever poetry classmates: Olga Moskvina, Liza Flum.

Thank you, mom and dad.

Thank you: Dani Li, Nathan Fulton, Adam Le, David Nash.

Thanks, Anton Khlevitt. For your unconditional love.

OTHER BOOKS FROM TUPELO PRESS

Silver Road: Essays, Maps & Calligraphies (memoir), Kazim Ali
A Certain Roughness in Their Syntax (poems), Jorge Aulicino, translated
   by Judith Filc
Another English: Anglophone Poems from Around the World (anthology),
   edited by Catherine Barnett and Tiphanie Yanique
gentlessness (poems), Dan Beachy-Quick
Personal Science (poems), Lillian-Yvonne Bertram
Almost Human (poems), Thomas Centolella
Hammer with No Master (poems), René Char, translated by Nancy
   Naomi Carlson
Land of Fire (poems), Mario Chard
New Cathay: Contemporary Chinese Poetry (anthology), edited by
   Ming Di
Gossip and Metaphysics: Russian Modernist Poetry and Prose (anthology),
   edited by Katie Farris, Ilya Kaminsky, and Valzhyna Mort
Poverty Creek Journal (memoir), Thomas Gardner
Leprosarium (poems), Lise Goett
My Immaculate Assassin (novel), David Huddle
Dancing in Odessa (poems), Ilya Kaminsky
Third Voice (poems), Ruth Ellen Kocher
Marvels of the Invisible (poems), Jenny Molberg
Canto General (poems), Pablo Neruda, translated by Mariela Griffor and
   Jeffrey Levine
The Ladder (poems), Alan Michael Parker
Ex-Voto (poems), Adélia Prado, translated by Ellen Doré Watson
The Life Beside This One (poems), Lawrence Raab
Intimate: An American Family Photo Album (hybrid memoir),
   Paisley Rekdal
Dirt Eaters (poems), Eliza Rotterman
Good Bones (poems), Maggie Smith
Swallowing the Sea (essays), Lee Upton
feast gently (poems), G. C. Waldrep
Legends of the Slow Explosion: Eleven Modern Lives (essays),
   Baron Wormser
Ordinary Misfortunes (poems), Emily Jungmin Yoon

See our complete list at www.tupelopress.org